Bugs in My Backyard

I See Walking Sticks

By Julia Jaske

 I see a walking stick.

I see a walking stick exploring.

4   I see a walking stick hanging.

I see a walking stick hiding.

 I see a green walking stick.

I see a brown walking stick.

I see a blue walking stick.

I see a walking stick camouflaging.

I see a walking stick smelling.

I see a walking stick eating.

I see a walking stick climbing.

I see a walking stick saying hello!

Word List

walking	blue
stick	camouflaging
exploring	smelling
hanging	eating
hiding	climbing
green	saying
brown	hello

72 Words

I see a walking stick.

I see a walking stick exploring.

I see a walking stick hanging.

I see a walking stick hiding.

I see a green walking stick.

I see a brown walking stick.

I see a blue walking stick.

I see a walking stick camouflaging.

I see a walking stick smelling.

I see a walking stick eating.

I see a walking stick climbing.

I see a walking stick saying hello!

Published in the United States of America by Cherry Lake Publishing Group
Ann Arbor, Michigan
www.cherrylakepublishing.com

Book Designer: Melinda Millward

Photo Credits: ©Mark Brandon/Shutterstock.com, front cover, 1, 4, 6, 7; ©Eric Isselee/
Shutterstock.com, back cover, 14; ©Ratchanee Sawasdijira/Shutterstock.com, 2; ©HTWE/
Shutterstock.com, 3; ©Arend Trent/Shutterstock.com, 5; ©kurt_G/Shutterstock.com, 8; ©ideation90/
Shutterstock.com, 9; ©Gabriel Phphy/Shutterstock.com, 10; ©LFRabanedo/Shutterstock.com, 11;
©Will Figueiredo/Shutterstock.com, 12; ©David W. Leindecker/Shutterstock.com, 13

Cherry Blossom Press is an imprint of Cherry Lake Publishing Group.

Library of Congress Cataloging-in-Publication Data

Names: Jaske, Julia, author.
Title: I see walking sticks / Julia Jaske.
Description: Ann Arbor, Michigan : Cherry Lake Publishing, 2022. | Series: Bugs in my backyard |
     Audience: Grades K-1
Identifiers: LCCN 2021036413 (print) | LCCN 2021036414 (ebook) | ISBN 9781534198876
     (paperback) | ISBN 9781668905777 (ebook) | ISBN 9781668901458 (pdf)
Subjects: LCSH: Stick insects—Juvenile literature.
Classification: LCC QL509.5 .J37 2022 (print) | LCC QL509.5 (ebook) | DDC 595.7/29—dc23
LC record available at https://lccn.loc.gov/2021036413
LC ebook record available at https://lccn.loc.gov/2021036414

Cherry Lake Publishing Group would like to acknowledge the work of the Partnership for 21st
Century Learning, a Network of Battelle for Kids. Please visit http://www.battelleforkids.org/
networks/p21 for more information.

Printed in the United States of America
Corporate Graphics